# Rookie

## Read-About® Geography

# California

## By Sarah De Capua

**Consultant**
Nanci Vargus, Ed.D.
Primary Multiage Teacher
Decatur Township Schools, Indianapolis, Indiana

**Children's Press®**
A Division of Scholastic Inc.
New York   Toronto   London   Auckland   Sydney
Mexico City   New Delhi   Hong Kong
Danbury, Connecticut

Designer: Herman Adler Design
Photo Researcher: Caroline Anderson
The photo on the cover shows the coast of California in Monterey County.

**Library of Congress Cataloging-in-Publication Data**

De Capua, Sarah.
 California / by Sarah de Capua.
    p. cm. — (Rookie read-about geography)
 Includes index.
 Summary: Introduces the geography, animals, tourist sites, and other facts about America's westernmost state.
  ISBN 0-516-22667-3 (lib. bdg.)     0-516-27492-9 (pbk.)
  1. California—Juvenile literature. 2. California—Geography—Juvenile literature. [1. California.] I. Title. II. Series.
  F861.3 .D43 2002
  917.94—dc21

                                    2002005491

Do you know where you can find the Golden Gate Bridge?

It is in the state of
California! Find California
on this map. It is located
in the western part of the
country.

CANADA

WASHINGTON

OREGON

IDAHO

MONTANA

NORTH DAKOTA

SOUTH DAKOTA

WYOMING

NEBRASKA

MINNESOTA

MICHIGAN

WISCONSIN

IOWA

NEVADA

UTAH

COLORADO

KANSAS

CALIFORNIA

ARIZONA

NEW MEXICO

OKLAHOMA

ARKANSAS

ILLINOIS

INDIANA

MISSOURI

KENTUCKY

TENNESSEE

TEXAS

LOUISIANA

MISSISSIPPI

ALABAMA

GEORGIA

FLORIDA

NEW HAMPSHIRE

VERMONT

MAINE

NEW YORK

MASSACHUSETTS

RHODE ISLAND

PENNSYLVANIA

CONNECTICUT

OHIO

NEW JERSEY

DELAWARE

WEST VIRGINIA

MARYLAND

VIRGINIA

Washington, D.C.

NORTH CAROLINA

SOUTH CAROLINA

ALASKA

CANADA

MEXICO

HAWAII

North

West

East

South

5

Many different kinds
of land can be found
in California. There are
mountains, farmland,
deserts, and forests.

There are two great mountain ranges in California. They are the Sierra Nevada and the Cascade.

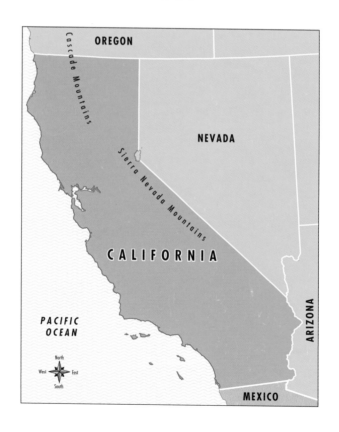

Mount Whitney is in the
Sierra Nevada mountain
range. It is the highest
point in California.

California's farmland is found east of the Sierra Nevada mountains. Fruits, vegetables, dairy products, and livestock come from this rich land.

11

The lowest point in the United States is called Badwater. It is located in Death Valley. Death Valley is part of the Mojave (mo-HAH-vee) Desert in southern California.

Northern California's forests are filled with giant trees called sequoia (si-KOY-ah) and redwood. They are some of the oldest and largest trees in the world.

The redwood is California's state tree.

California is next to the Pacific Ocean. Fishermen catch salmon, swordfish, shrimp, and squid in the water near California's coast.

Los Angeles

18

Los Angeles is California's largest city. Sacramento is the state capital.

California's other major cities include San Jose (hoh-ZAY), San Francisco (fran-SIS-ko), and San Diego.

Some people who work in California's cities have jobs in the computer industry. Others work in factories where they make aircraft, spacecraft, or cars.

21

Most of our country's dairy
products come from farms
in California. Grapes are
an important crop. They are
grown in vineyards. Grapes
are used to make wine.

It can be cold and snowy
in northern California.

It is warm all year long
in southern California.

The California Quail
is California's state bird.
It lives in the forest.

Desert animals include
jackrabbits, lizards, and
rattlesnakes.

What is your favorite
place in California?

# Words You Know

Death Valley

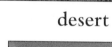

desert

farmland

Golden Gate Bridge

30

Mount Whitney

Pacific Ocean

redwood

vineyard

# Index

## About the Author

Sarah De Capua is an author and editor of children's books.
She resides in Colorado.

## Photo Credits

Photographs © 2002: David R. Frazier: 28 (Mike Penney), 6 bottom right, 6
bottom left, 11 top, 11 bottom, 12, 15, 18, 25, 30 top left, 30 top right, 31
bottom left; PhotoEdit: 17, 31 top right (Tony Freeman), 21 (Spencer Grant), 27
(Bonnie Kamin); Robert Fried Photography: 3, 6 top left, 6 top right, 14, 22, 24,
30 bottom left, 30 bottom right, 31 bottom right; Robert Holmes Photography:
9, 31 top left; Terry Donnelly: cover; Visuals Unlimited/John C. Muegge: 26.

Maps by Bob Italiano

# Journey to Hong Kong

## by Erin Cameron

Glenview, Illinois • Boston, Massachusetts • Chandler, Arizona • Upper Saddle River, New Jersey

**Phototgraphs**

Every effort has been made to secure permission and provide appropriate credit for photographic material. The publisher deeply regrets any omission and pledges to correct errors called to its attention in subsequent editions.

Unless otherwise acknowledged, all photographs are the property of Pearson.

Photo locators denoted as follows: Top (T), Center (C), Bottom (B), Left (L), Right (R), Background (Bkgd)

**CVR** © Jon Bower Hong Kong/Alamy Images; **1** Getty Images; **3** © Richard Cummins/ SuperStock; **4** Texas State University-San Marcos; **5,19** Texas Mathworks; **7** (T) Cubo Images/Robert Harding World Imagery, (B) Getty Images; **8** © Jon Bower Hong Kong/ Alamy Images; **10** (T) Getty Images, (B) Westend61/Punchstock; **11** ©Redchopsticks /Alamy; **12** J Yip/CPL/Panoramic Images; **13-16** Amanda Voigt; **21** (T) © Paul Yeung/ Reuters/Corbis, (B) Getty Images; **22** © Lester Lefkowitz/Corbis.

ISBN 13: 978-0-328-39482-1
ISBN 10:    0-328-39482-3

3 4 5 6 7 8 9 10 V0N4 13 12 11 10
CC1

Seventh-grader Bobby Shen was a boy who enjoyed a challenge. In his hometown of Sugar Land, Texas, just outside of Houston, Bobby liked competing in math contests. Two hundred miles away, in Austin—Texas's capital city—Catherine Liu and Alexandra Ilic were just as competitive and as skilled at math. The girls attended the same middle school, but eighth-grader Catherine was a year ahead of Alexandra. At another Austin school, seventh-grader Kevin Tian had sharpened his math skills in contests and **competitions** too. Everyone except Bobby knew each other from earlier math contests and camps they had taken part in.

In the summer of 2007, these four students took the journey of a lifetime, to compete in the 11th Primary Math World Contest in Hong Kong, China.

Texans Alexandra Ilic, Catherine Liu, and Kevin Tian all came from Austin, shown below. Bobby Shen was from Sugar Land.

# Getting There

The journey to Hong Kong began with a math test—naturally. In the fall of 2006, teachers from the math department at Texas State University sent out a test to middle-school teachers across the state. Students who wanted to try their hand at working these **challenging** problems took the test. Thirty or so high-scoring students would get a chance to take part in a summer math camp at Texas State University in San Marcos. The four top-scoring students would travel to Hong Kong to compete in the worldwide math contest.

In February 2007, Bobby Shen, Catherine Liu, Alexandra Ilic, and Kevin Tian learned that they were the four top-scoring students.

**Bobby, Catherine, Alexandra, and Kevin attended Mathworks summer camp at Texas State University in San Marcos, Texas.**

The team posed for pictures with the mayor of San Marcos and their coaches, and local newspapers carried the story.

At that summer's Mathworks camp at Texas State University, the four had fun, but they worked hard too. They **renewed** friendships with counselors and students they had met earlier summers. They also learned creative ways to solve problems and practiced working together as the team they needed to become.

Each person had his or her own strengths. Bobby was very focused and worked fast. Catherine was skilled at logic problems and remained calm under pressure. Alexandra worked number problems like a machine, almost never making mistakes. Kevin had a sharp mind and worked well with everyone.

Working as a team would be different from working alone. Sometimes, working alone was easier.

To win in Hong Kong, though, each person would have to make use of everyone's strengths instead of only his or her own. As a team, they could attack more difficult problems and also divide up the work to solve problems faster. And they could double-check one another's work and share ideas.

# Hong Kong

On the morning of Thursday, July 12, the San Marcos Mathworks team left for Hong Kong, along with team leaders Hiroko Warshauer and Amanda Voigt.

The trip to Hong Kong was long—19 hours in all. The plane took off at 7:25 in the morning, as the sun climbed into the Texas sky. As the jet traveled east, it carried its passengers through 12 of the world's 24 time zones. Each zone was one hour ahead of the one before it. This means that the time in Hong Kong is 13 hours ahead of the time in Austin. When they touched down at Hong Kong International Airport, it was 3:15 P.M. on Friday. At the same moment, clocks in Austin would have read 2:15 A.M.

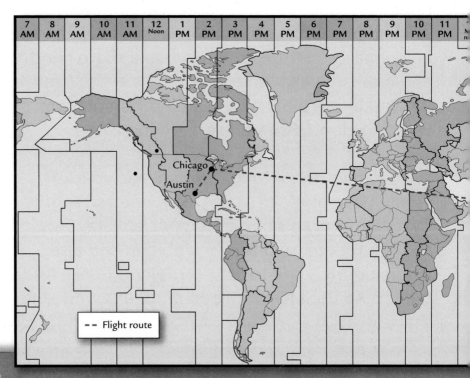

Finally, they stepped off the airplane into Hong Kong International Airport, stretching their legs and blinking with **exhaustion**. The airport, like much of Hong Kong, seemed modern and very busy. High walls of glass and steel let sunlight shine into open, airy buildings. It could have been an airport in any large, Western city, except for signs printed with Chinese characters.

The Hong Kong International Airport opened in the late 1990s and is one of the busiest airports in the world.

Because Earth makes one complete turn every 24 hours, sunlight and darkness fall at different times in different places. To make timekeeping simpler, countries use a system of 24 time zones. Each zone is one hour later than the zone immediately west of it.

July in Hong Kong is as hot and damp as a steam bath. The region lies near Earth's equator. Even the group from Texas, where summers are famously hot, plucked at their sweaty T-shirts in the heat of the Hong Kong summer.

Hong Kong is the name of both a region of China and an island city within that region. The region known as Hong Kong has more than 230 islands, and the city of Hong Kong stands on one of them.

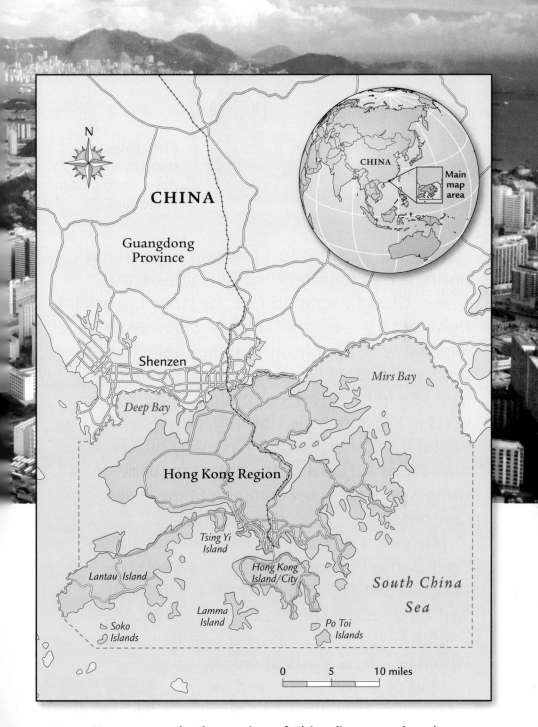

**N**

**CHINA**

Guangdong
Province

Shenzen

*Deep Bay*

*Mirs Bay*

Hong Kong Region

CHINA

Main
map
area

*Tsing Yi
Island*

*Lantau Island*

*Hong Kong
Island/City*

*South China
Sea*

*Lamma
Island*

▷ *Soko
Islands*

*Po Toi
Islands*

0      5      10 miles

Hong Kong names both a region of China (in orange) and an
island city within that region.

Glass-covered skyscrapers of Hong Kong glisten in the sunlight.

The first thing visitors to Hong Kong Island notice is that it glitters like sunshine on the ocean. Glass skyscrapers line the streets, sparkling right up to the edge of the sea. Sidewalks are jammed with people, all rushing busily to one place or another. Most of them look like they could be in New York or London because they dress in Western-style clothing. Most speak either English or Chinese, which has many different dialects, or versions of the same language. In Hong Kong, the most common Chinese dialect is Cantonese.

Everywhere a person looks, colorful, lighted signs printed in both Chinese and English advertise luggage, tailors, or food. Chinese writing does not use the same alphabet that English writing uses. Chinese characters are whole words, or parts of words, instead of letters that stand for sounds. For example, the Cantonese word for taxi, shown at the right, is pronounced "deek/SEE."

Most people in Hong Kong wear Western-style clothing and speak Cantonese.

# Sightseeing in Hong Kong

Before the math competition, the team had two days to get used to being in a different culture and time zone. Their bodies still felt as if they were on Austin time. When they had landed at 3:00 P.M. in Hong Kong, they felt like it was 2:00 A.M., or the middle of the night. This feeling is called *jet lag*, and it happens a lot to people who travel across time zones. The best cure is to give the body a day or two to adjust.

During this time, the San Marcos team met other contestants from around the world. Dozens of countries sent teams to the Primary Math World Contest, including Singapore, China, Japan, South Africa, Australia, Mexico, and two other teams from the U.S.

The Hong Kong skyline is often compared to the skyline of New York because both have so many skyscrapers.

The team also used these days to see the sights of Hong Kong. They rode a ferry across the harbor, once filled with sampans. Now modern fishing boats, ferries, and luxury yachts cruise these waters.

They rode up to Victoria Peak, the highest mountain on Hong Kong Island. From there, they gazed down on the city's glistening skyline.

The team visited the University of China and the Tsing Ma Bridge, an enormous structure that stretches from Tsing Yi Island to Ma Wan Island. At a little more than three-quarters of a mile, it's one of the longest bridges in the world and carries both cars and trains on its double-decker span.

Students pose outside the shark aquarium.

While team leaders took photos of bridges and harbors, Bobby, Catherine, Alexandra, and Kevin were more interested in getting to know each other better. Over the next two days, the four spent a lot of time playing card games and talking. They even invented their own role-playing game, which they named "Double Mafia." In it, players took on roles, such as criminal, healer, or storyteller.

In all of their games, Bobby showed lots of energy and had good ideas. Catherine could be counted on to notice details. Bright and friendly Alexandra proved that, like Bobby, she could think fast. Kevin, who enjoyed telling stories, showed that he was a creative problem-solver. Knowing each other in this way would prove helpful to them in the team contest ahead.

The Texas team spent time getting to know each other better. Here, Alexandra, Bobby, and Kevin talk.

# Competition Day Arrives

On the day of the competition, team members woke up early. They were excited about the contest but not nervous. With hours to burn, they played card games and talked some more. Finally, a bus picked up the group and carried them to Po Leung Kuk Grandmont Primary School. They tramped up the stairs, some joking, some quiet, but all of them ready.

The time had come to do what they did best. The first part of the competition required team members to solve problems individually. These were tough problems, and competitors had a limited time to work them.

**The Primary Math World Competition took place at Grandmont Primary School.**

When everyone on the Texas team handed in their work and walked back down the stairs for lunch, they seemed **confident**. Questions and chatter bounced back and forth about how they had worked the problems and what answers they had reached.

Team leaders seemed sure that their team had done well. Still, they had an even tougher challenge ahead: the team test would begin after lunch.

For this part of the contest, each team would solve a number of extremely difficult problems together. They would need to use **logic** and new ways of thinking to work out the solutions.

Team members during the competition.
From left to right: Catherine, Kevin, Bobby,
and Alexandra.

First, each team received several problems to divide among themselves. Team members had to work through at least one problem on their own; then the team had to work together.

They had to solve two problems as a group. **Cooperation** was important. They listened to each other and shared ideas. If members disagreed about how best to solve a problem, they remembered that there is often more than one way to reach a solution. They double-checked their own answers and then one another's.

By the middle of the afternoon, the contest was over. Members of the San Marcos team believed they had done well—but had other teams done better?

Returning to the hotel to relax for a bit, the four competitors and their chaperones prepared for the evening's events—a banquet, the awards ceremony, and then a talent show.

**In the team event, each student worked at least one problem alone. The team decided how to solve the other problems.**

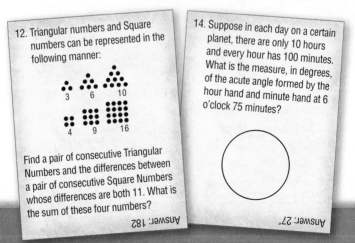

12. Triangular numbers and Square numbers can be represented in the following manner:

3    6    10

4    9    16

Find a pair of consecutive Triangular Numbers and the differences between a pair of consecutive Square Numbers whose differences are both 11. What is the sum of these four numbers?

Answer: 182

14. Suppose in each day on a certain planet, there are only 10 hours and every hour has 100 minutes. What is the measure, in degrees, of the acute angle formed by the hour hand and minute hand at 6 o'clock 75 minutes?

Answer: 27°

# The Po Leung Kuk Cup

After the banquet, the hall began to fill with excitement and **anticipation**. As teams waited to hear the results, the babble of young voices rose higher and higher.

Bobby, Catherine, Alexandra, and Kevin knew they had done well, but they were **perfectionists**. Questions nagged at them: Could they have found a faster way to solve the last problem? Was their work on the first problem clear?

The team also knew that the other teams were tough competitors and would be hard to beat. The emcee spoke and then introduced all of the competing teams. Then, division by division, the names of winners were announced. Suspense mounted with each announcement.

The San Marcos team received top honors in the contest for non-Asian teams.

Finally, it was time to know who won in the San Marcos's team's division for non-Asian teams. Bobby, always full of energy, could hardly sit still. Even Catherine, the calm one, was excited. Then the words that they had not dared to hope for filled the hall: The San Marcos Mathworks team had won top honors! Their hard work had paid off.

The team was amazed. They would take home the Po Leung Kuk Cup, top award for non-Asian teams!

After that, their evening was all about having fun and cheering for the other teams. At the talent show following the awards ceremony, the jubilant San Marcos team did a "chicken dance" with so much spirit that everyone in the room stood up and danced with them.

Bobby, Catherine, Alexandra, Kevin, and the team leaders boarded the airplane for their long flight home on Wednesday, July 18. Between meals and games and sharing puzzles, they laughed and chattered about their adventures. Then, back home in Texas, the four young people went their separate ways for the rest of the summer.

Their shared competitive spirit and love of math might bring them all together again. But together or not, they will always share memories of an unforgettable journey to Hong Kong.

Celebrating their victory, the group visited Hong Kong Disneyland on Tuesday, the day after the contest. It was a good way to say good-bye to Hong Kong.

## Flying Home

Here's a math problem for you to try. The team left Hong Kong on July 18th at around 1:00 in the afternoon. Their total travel time was 23 hours. Can you figure out what time it was when they arrived back in Austin? Don't forget the 13-hour time difference!

# Now Try This

The San Marcos team was able to learn about Hong Kong by meeting people and visiting the region. If a worldwide contest were held near where you live, what do you think visitors from other countries would want to see? Write a one-day schedule for a group of students your age who are visiting from another country. Include details about where they would go and what they would want to do.

**Where might foreign students want to go if they visited your community?**

1. Use a newspaper or community Web site to help you think about attractions in your area. If you have access to the Internet, search for your local visitors' bureau. Ask yourself, "What is special about my community?"

2. Talk with friends about how you like to spend extra time in your area. Would students from another part of the world be interested in the same things you enjoy?

3. Make a list of the things that you think students from another country would find interesting in your community. Make a note of how long each activity would take.

4. Write out a one-day schedule for your visitors, from after-breakfast until dinner time. Include restaurants you think the visitors would enjoy.

5. Share the schedule with your class. Explain why you think the activities and places you chose would interest students from another country.

# Glossary

anticipation *n.* act of looking forward to; expectation

challenging *adj.* difficult

competition *n.* a contest

confident *adj.* having a firm belief in yourself; being certain or sure of something

cooperation *n.* act or process of working together; united effort or labor

exhaustion *n.* a feeling of being very tired

logic *n.* science of proof and of reasoning

perfectionists *n.* people who insist that things be perfect

renewed *v.* made new again